contents

jobs in the food industry

Whatever you eat or drink is a product of the food industry. The term 'food industry' covers every stage in the process from growing crops and rearing animals to the finished product on the supermarket shelf.

Job opportunities

Job opportunities exist on many levels and range from those which require few qualifications to those which make use of the most advanced academic qualifications and skills.

Where are the opportunities? They are:
* in research and development, including **market research** and **test kitchens**
* behind the scenes, for example, in administration, in finance, marketing and purchasing
* in warehouses and maintenance units
* in production (including manufacturing processes)
* in creative and experimental departments (including nutrition, product design and development, quality assurance and food science)
* in technical departments (including increased computerization – information technology (IT) specialists are some of the most important people in the industry)
* in distribution and transport (called **logistics**)
* in the maintenance of hygiene, health and safe working methods.

Logistics

Distribution and logistics involves organizing the delivery of products from where they are grown or manufactured to the retail outlets from which they will

▼ Some food products must be kept fresh, and chilled if necessary, while being transported from the factory to the supermarket.

be sold. The products must be kept fresh and those, which are chilled or frozen, must be kept in that state. Logistics is a complex part of food production. It involves planning and organizing how to get raw materials to the factory as well as how to distribute the resulting food products from the factory to sales outlets, such as supermarkets and shops. Computers are used a great deal in this section of the food industry, so people involved must be computer literate.

Sales

The food industry is a competitive market. There is always a **competitor** who would like their product to be bought instead of yours. Being a successful sales person involves being very creative and determined and having the ability to persuade people to buy the products with which you are working. It is important also to have faith in the products. Normally sales people work in a team, but each member has to be able to understand the needs of retailers and consumers and know how to meet them.

Manufacturing

This is the heart of the food industry. It involves turning ingredients into food products that are safe and tasty to eat and are commercially successful.

Food is a complex material – one item of food has lots of chemicals in it, all of which interact with each other. This means that an important part of food manufacture is ensuring that any interaction between the various chemicals makes products that are safe to eat as well as appetizing.

People and machines are important in the manufacturing process. The people involved must have a good 'team spirit'. Production involves the following:
- planning and designing the process
- operating machinery
- supervising other workers
- engineering (including designing and installing machinery and making sure they run smoothly).

Buying

Buying is a crucial part of the whole food production industry. Without good quality raw materials the final product will never meet the quality aspect of the **specification**.

Case study

Lien Ha is an operational support worker at Coca-Cola Enterprises.

'The cans of Coca-Cola I help distribute are manufactured in Milton Keynes. Our main customers are the UK supermarkets such as Tesco and ASDA who channel their orders through our customer service team in Nottingham. These orders are entered on our computer systems and they reach me about 36 hours later.

'I co-ordinate the logistics of delivering the stock. This involves arranging the arrival and departure of lorries to collect the drinks cans - ideally without causing too much congestion at our warehouse. I also ensure we have enough cans on site to fill the delivery. Each lorry load contains 26 'pallets' - that's 74,880 cans!

'If there are any problems with the order I tell customer services who inform the relevant supermarket. To meet customer demand the business is open around the clock. That means that I do sometimes have to work night shifts.'

large scale, small scale

This is the story of a company, which started making jams and preserves on a small scale and gradually increased its output to produce many different products on a large scale. The name given to the products is 'Tiptree', so called because Tiptree in Essex is where the factory is based. The company's name is Wilkin and Son.

▼ *Teams of pickers are used to harvest fruit for jam production.*

Their approach

The company has always grown much of the fruit used for the preserves on its own farms. They have also extended their range of products to fit in with the seasons. They work on a four-season cycle. For example, the production of marmalade takes place when Seville oranges are at their best in January.

Other developments

In industry a crucial part of commercial success is the fact that employees and machinery should always be in use. This is one of the reasons why Tiptree started to make Christmas puddings – they fill a gap in their production cycle. The puddings are produced in November ready for sale at Christmas.

Principles of jam-making

Regardless of the scale of jam production, the principles to follow are the same:
- use best-quality ingredients in the right proportion
- boil for the required length of time at the appropriate temperature
- fill sterilized jars with the exact amount
- cap and seal jars.

The industrial process

1. Selection, grading and cleaning of fruit – at Tiptree fruit is sorted by hand as it enters the factory.
2. Weighing and measuring of ingredients.
3. Boiling – this removes excess water to concentrate the mixture, strengthens the flavour, prevents the formation of large sugar crystals that would make the jam 'gritty', and destroys yeasts and moulds.

4. Filling the jars – at Tiptree jars are filled at a rate of up to 70,000 a day. The jars are first cleaned, usually by **compressed air** which flushes out any foreign material. The jars are then heated and placed on a carousel.

5. Finish, testing and inspection – the jars are capped immediately after filling. Care is taken to make sure air is removed from the jar and that there is a good seal. The jars are then cooled by jets of water, care being taken to avoid too rapid cooling, which would crack the glass. Inspections for quality are carried out by specialized people.

6. Packing and distribution – at Tiptree, up-to-date machinery labels and packs 300 jars per minute, whilst alongside skilled workers pack smaller export orders by hand.

Filling is an automated process, where the exact amount of jam is deposited into the jar as it travels along the carousel.

Keeping up with changing tastes

This is an important part of being commercially successful. Consumer tastes change and create the need for new or adapted products. Tiptree Fruit Spreads are an example of such a product. These meet the consumers' need for less sweet jams. They are sold in jars just like jam and taste of fresh fruit. They contain 45 grams only of sugar per 100 grams, compared with about 75 grams sugar to 100 grams fruit for strawberry jam and 100 grams sugar to 100 grams fruit for loganberry jam.

systems in food

Systems are crucial for food production. They help to control the processes so that the wastage of materials, time and money is kept to a minimum. Systems have three parts:

1. Input is what is put into the system – the ingredients or raw materials.
2. Process is what happens inside the system – the production.
3. Output is what comes out of the system – the product.

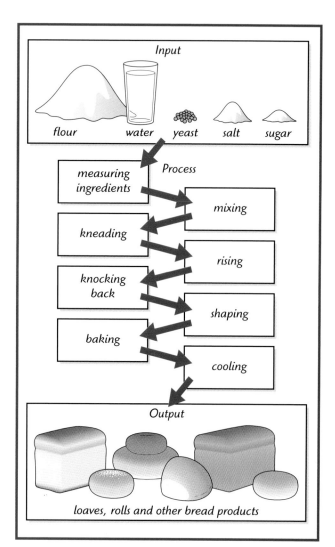

▲ A simple way of understanding systems is shown here in relation to bread-making.

Specification

People who design systems must consider both input and output, and what must happen in the process in order to produce the quality and quantity of product required. These people are sometimes called systems engineers. Their task is to design the best systems to ensure a successful output. Their work is based on the description of what the product must be like – the **specification**. This is provided by research carried out during the product development processes. This includes finding out the proportions and combinations of ingredients that will produce the best example of the product and the manufacturing processes that will produce the best results.

Sub-systems

When systems are designed, each aspect of the process is divided into smaller parts, which are called sub-systems. An example would be a coffee bar in a busy train station. Customers would normally require fast service in this situation so the system must be effective and efficient. This is achieved by the existence of a number of sub-systems within the system. The following sub-systems are in operation:

1. The counter – customers give their order at the counter.
2. The production – information from the counter is passed to the process area where, for example, a supply of hot water, coffee, milk and clean cups will be available.
3. The service area – the final products are taken to the service counter, where the customer pays.

The information provided by each of the above is called **feedback** information. It ensures that the system is effective and efficient by feeding to the appropriate sub-system information about what is required.

Closed-loop, open-loop

This type of provision of information within a system creates a closed-loop system, so called because all the feedback information remains within the system. The station coffee bar is an example of a closed-loop system, where a continuous supply of coffee is required. The same processes occur over and over again with information about demand and supply flowing in both directions of the system, that is from input to output and from output to input.

Another system is the open-loop control system. This is where the information moves in one direction only – from input to output. There is no feedback in an open-loop system. The diagram of the bread-making process is an example of this type of system.

Information gathering

The checking and monitoring of activities are carried out by both people and machines. A very simple example is a fast food outlet. The information about the number of people ordering specific dishes at the counter is fed back to the cooking (process) area and the required number of portions is produced.

The parts of a system which people use are called **user interfaces**. In this example the user interface is the counter at which the customer orders the food. Interfaces can be human or machine. **Vending machines** are examples of machine interfaces. When human decision-making is not part of a system, it is called a hard system.

A closed-loop, hard system

A simple example is a freezer which has to be kept below a certain temperature, or the food will deteriorate and become unsafe to eat. A sensor monitors the temperature and provides the feedback necessary for effective temperature control.

In this example the sensor is **calibrated**, usually by a human engineer. The visual display shows the temperature at which the freezer is working. If the system goes out of control, a bleeper may sound to alert someone that all is not well, or the system may be designed to adjust itself to the correct temperature.

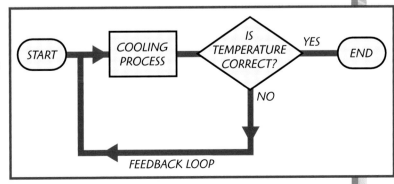

computer control

Control systems are used to ensure that a high-quality product which fully meets the **specification** is produced. When food is prepared at home or on a very small scale, the cook is the control system. This may involve:

- weighing ingredients accurately, according to the recipe
- deciding when the consistency, **viscosity**, size and amount are right
- selecting appropriate temperatures
- deciding when the product is cooked, browned, chilled or frozen sufficiently.

In large-scale production it is mostly computers that do the controlling. Computer-aided Manufacture (CAM) is the name used for this.

Any piece of equipment that works mechanically or electrically has to have a control system as part of its operation, even if it is just a simple on/off switch. Electronic sensors are used in food processing to detect the changes that take place as the food is processed. They are a key feature of most systems used in large-scale food production.

Electronic sensors

The following are some examples of electronic sensors used in the food industry:

- Metal detectors identify changes in the magnetic field to detect any metal objects in food that should not be there.
- Reflectometers are used to monitor colour changes during the cooking of food. They work by measuring the colour and intensity (strength) of light reflected from an object.

- Thermocouples and thermistors monitor temperature. For example, they control oven temperature.
- Load cells are used to monitor weight. They give an electrical signal in relation to how much they are loaded in relation to the weight required. For example, as a mixer is being filled with an ingredient, it puts a load on the cell. The cell gives a signal to the control system, which indicates how full or empty the mixer is.
- Photo-cells are used to check the level of contents in a container. They are light sensitive and can detect if anything is in the beam of light. If the beam of light can reach the photo-cell then there is nothing in the way.

Information from sensors is received at a **central processing unit (CPU)**. The information is recorded in a number of ways:

1. Lights coming on or a buzzer sounding.
2. A graph where the datum is continually changing.
3. A dial with a needle which moves across it.
4. A digital read-out with numbers.

Sensors in the test kitchen

To check that the instructions printed on the package for reheating a 'ready meal' are accurate and will mean the product is safe, the product is heated in a microwave in a **test kitchen**. Each component of the product has a colour-coded **optic fibre** inserted into it which registers the internal temperature. This is monitored by a simple software package on a computer. The microwave is attached to a computer system, which

▲ ▶ *These photographs show how the internal temperatures of a product can be monitored using sensors attached to a computer.*

prints the internal temperature of all the components onto a graph on the screen. When the appropriate levels are reached, the graph freezes into a still form which can then be printed.

Computer Integrated Manufacture

Computers are also used to link together the systems in a food production system. This is called computer integrated manufacture (CIM). The whole production process is controlled by computer from a central point. Bread production is a good example. The amount and type of flour, the cooking temperature and the cooling times can all be regulated. An engineer, responsible for making sure everything runs smoothly, checks the computer print-out at intervals, locates any fault in the system and also checks that the right ingredients are being used for the different varieties of bread in production.

The computer control covers:
• ingredient weights
• the flow rate through the system of ingredients or a mixture ,
• the temperature
• the **pH**
• the moisture content
• the pressure
• the speed of a conveyor belt
• viscosity and consistency.

Computer Aided Design

This makes use of drawing and graphics packages on a computer. It allows the designer to check and control all the relevant aspects of a projected design. CAD and CAM (computer aided manufacture) can be linked together very effectively to control all aspects of production, from package design to the quality-assured finished product.

critical control points

Critical control points (CCPs) are specific actions that are built into a food production system at stages where a risk exists or a hazard could occur. CCPs can be part of a practice, a particular procedure in a process, a particular process or a place where a process takes place. All aspects of production and all working procedures and conditions must be included when an analysis of potential hazards is being carried out.

Hazard prevention

CCPs are installed to prevent hazards occurring in production. A hazard is anything that is potentially harmful to the consumer and therefore undesirable in the food product. For example:

- food contamination with foreign objects, such as metal or glass, pests or harmful chemicals
- growth and survival of **micro-organisms** in the product
- production of toxins in the product as a result of micro-organism growth.

In the pasteurization process, for example, a critical control point is installed to ensure the appropriate temperature is achieved and held for the required length of time to kill any unwanted micro-organisms present.

Safety controls

CCPs must ensure that there are adequate safety controls in place and that they are monitored to check they are working effectively. The assessment, control and monitoring procedures are reviewed periodically and whenever food operations change. The actions involved in how control is achieved at each CCP must be described specifically. This description becomes the criteria for particular operations.

Criteria

The aspects that the criteria cover are:

- physical, such as time and temperature
- chemical, such as the concentration of salt in a solution or measuring the **pH** of a solution
- biological, such as the detection of pests or other organisms
- sensory, as in appearance, colour and consistency.

A list of criteria are placed in prominent places in a factory next to the relevant area to remind staff, particularly those who have responsibility for that part of the process. The criteria should be easily understood, realistic and sensible.

◀ *Checking the temperature of milk during the production of cheese.*

Information like this should be available wherever food is produced or kept. ▶

Criteria must provide a high level of assurance that effective control of hazards is taking place and that the controls should either eliminate the hazard or reduce it to a safe, acceptable level. They are developed according to their usefulness, cost and manageability.

HACCP

The historical background to this system is said to come from space exploration. It is essential that food to be eaten in space is 100 per cent safe and will not cause sickness. It is said that a long list of possible hazards was prepared in the early days of planning space exploration. Extensive checks for bacteria, pests and foreign material took place and all methods of processing were carried out to eliminate hazards. In summary, the process consisted of hazard analysis (HA) and prevention and elimination of hazards at particular points during processing and storage by CCPs in the system. The whole approach was given the title HACCP.

What is the link between hazard and risk? The chance of a hazard causing harm or damage is called a risk. It is possible to work out how big a risk is by assessing the likely harm or damage that might occur. This is called risk assessment. Risk control

What are the basic temperature requirements?

The Regulations state that foods which need temperature control for safety must be held either:

Hot:

at or above a minimum temperature of 63°C.

Chilled:

at or below a maximum temperature of 8°C.

▲ 63°C

▼ 8°C

Certain foods may be exempt from these requirements and there is room for flexibility in certain circumstances. Details are given in this booklet.

is the action taken to make sure that harm or damage is less likely to occur.

High-risk areas

Certain parts of a food production process carry a high degree of risk. For example, products which have been prepared and cooked, but not yet packaged, could become contaminated. The area set aside for covering and packing a product is a high-risk area as a result. The control points placed in the covering and packing areas must take account of this. The controls that are in place must ensure that risk to food safety is eliminated or reduced to a minimum.

Noon Products – a case study

The following industrial example of food production relates to a company which specializes in making chilled and frozen Indian ready meals. The company is called Noon Products plc. The basis for all their products is authentic Indian cooking. Product development starts with ideas from traditional domestic recipes which are scaled up to commercial quantities. Most products are based on chicken, lamb, prawns or vegetables, a sauce and rice.

A typical chicken and rice product has to go through various stages. Some of the production environment is identified as being a high risk area where the risk of contamination is at its highest. Other areas are identified as low risk.

Different clothing is required for the high and low risk areas:
- For the low risk area: jackets with blue pockets, black boots.
- For the high risk area: jackets with red pockets, white boots.

Blue hairnets, hats and disposable gloves must be worn in all areas. Blue is chosen because, as no food is coloured blue, if these items were to fall into the food accidentally during processing they would be seen immediately.

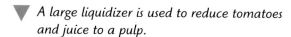

The spices are checked for quality and then weighed according to the specification.

A large liquidizer is used to reduce tomatoes and juice to a pulp.

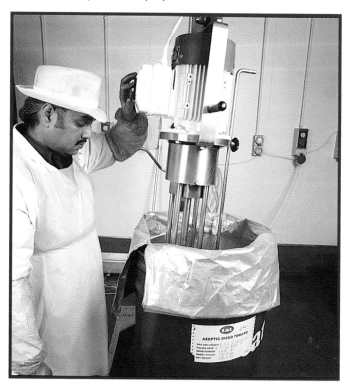

Diced raw chicken, coated in sauce, is placed on the wire conveyor belt which will take the chicken through the oven to be cooked. The temperature and time required are programmed into the system. The controls for one of the ovens can be seen at the top of the photo.

The sealed trays move along on a conveyor belt and pass through a metal detector. Each tray is also weighed. If metal is detected or the weight does not meet the specification that tray is automatically pushed into one of the reject areas. These have a lock on them to prevent the rejected trays being put back into the system.

High risk area

Cooked chicken and rice are weighed according to the specification and put into trays. Sauce is then added by machine. The machine has been programmed to deposit (called dumped in industry) the required amount of sauce into each pack.

Film is then placed over two trays and cut by a machine after which the trays are moved along by a belt and the edges of the film are sealed.

Low risk area

In the packing room trays are placed in a sleeve which is stamped with a 'use by' date and the sleeved products are delivered to the retailer. Green crates are used for delivery rather than cardboard boxes so that they can be returned to Noon who wash and clean them ready to use again.

Quality control

At Noon, quality control procedures ensure that:
- storage, cooking and cooling temperatures are appropriate for the safety of the product at every stage during processing
- all ingredients are weighed accurately, ratios checked and the correct amounts of sauce added to the product
- sealing and foreign body (e.g. metal) detection is carried out effectively
- meals are the correct weight and sleeved correctly.

Together, these control procedures provide the evidence that safe and consistent products are being made. This is called product assurance.

Pilau rice being cooked.

one-off production

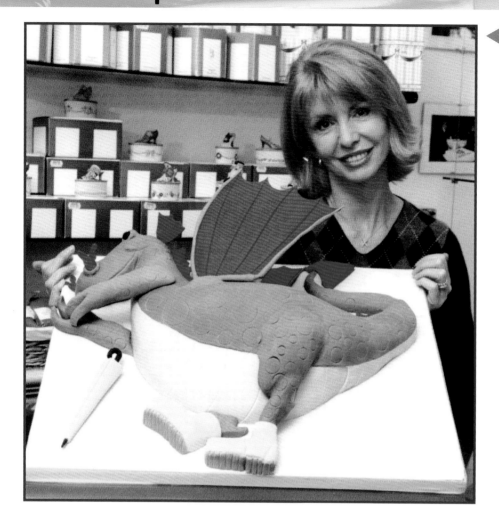

This photograph shows Jane Asher with one of the special cake designs that has been produced by the Jane Asher Party Cakes company.

Individual cakes

Jane Asher Party Cakes is an example of a company which produces hand-crafted cakes to order. Single items can be designed and produced according to the individual customer's requirements.

How does the company work?

The basic cake mixtures are made in large slabs. The mixtures include fruit and sponges in various flavours, including chocolate. The slabs of cake are cut into the shapes and sizes required by the individual design. Each cake is decorated and iced by hand by a highly skilled person. Appropriately sized boxes are used to pack each order. Great care is taken to make sure the boxes are strong enough to prevent damage. Cakes may be collected from the shop or they can be safely delivered by courier.

Why is this company so successful?

There are a number of reasons why the company is so successful. Jane Asher spotted a gap in the market for the one-off production of individually designed products. She then set about organizing a system which would produce a high-quality range of types and sizes of cakes. Another reason is the stress laid upon the fact that no **specification** is too small or too difficult.

Jane Asher Party Cakes also has a mail order section. Again the success of this is the way it is organized and marketed. Mail order allows people from all over the country to buy the products and have them personalized.

Home-made pies!

The Patchwork Traditional Food Company is an example of a company that makes good-quality products characteristic of home-style cooking. It specializes in patés, terrines and pies. The company was started ten years ago by Margaret Carter, who is a talented but untrained cook. She devised and tested recipes in her home kitchen and began selling her products to pubs nearby. The start-up cost was £9, which Margaret saved from her housekeeping money. The products are additive-free, without artificial colouring or flavouring.

The business progressed rapidly until eventually, it became necessary to move the business from Margaret's home to an industrial unit and then a huge, purpose-built factory. The product range has expanded but Margaret has always insisted that the ingredients must be fresh and also that raw materials must be obtained locally as often as possible.

The same way of working...

Despite the commercial scale of production the same recipes and processes are used in the factory as in Margaret's kitchen. The products are still hand-made, in small batches. Margaret says that as demand increases further she will just employ more people to meet the demand, but she will not change the method of production. In fact about 35 people are employed in the production of 2.5 tonnes of products per week.

...Ensures high quality

When twelve pies of a certain kind are made, twelve mixing bowls and twelve balls of pastry are lined up with twelve portions of weighed ingredients as part of the production process. This approach is Margaret's answer to ensuring that her products are both consistent and of high quality.

No supermarkets

The products are transported all over the UK and to Southern Ireland in refrigerated lorries to fulfill the many orders that arrive daily. Customers have expanded from pubs only to restaurants, delicatessens, butchers and food outlets. However, Patchwork does not supply large multi-national supermarkets because, to quote Margaret, 'Multiples would try to dictate price and quality, imbalance our cash flow and take business away from our loyal, smaller customers, with whom we have a natural connection.'

batch production

Batch production describes the process of making a number of the same products at the same time, using the same systems. In large-scale batch production conveyor belt systems are often used. However, batch production can be carried out on a variety of scales.

Domestic batch production covers the scaling-up of a particular recipe, such as that for a Victoria sandwich cake, so that more than one cake can be produced from the same recipe at the same time. It is a method of saving time, fuel and human energy. The amount of each ingredient is increased in the appropriate proportion to the other ingredients and the scaled-up mixture is prepared using the same method as for the original one-off amount. The mixture is then divided into the appropriate number of containers for baking. In a domestic situation products are often batch-baked and then stored in the freezer for use at a later stage.

At the baker's

In an independent baker's, the products are made in batches on a slightly larger scale. The doughs are made up in the required quantity and processed to make a variety of products. The baker estimates what will be sold and what consumers will require on any one day and produces accordingly. For example, on Fridays and Saturdays there may be a demand for

A baker must estimate the amount of bread that will be sold in one day before production can begin. ▶

more exotic breads and cakes because people usually have more time to enjoy something different at the weekend.

There is an increasing demand for special bread varieties, such as herb breads and Italian breads like ciabatta. The independent baker needs to meet its customers demands and has to be able to adapt its products accordingly.

Batch-baking principles

The principles of batch-baking cover:
- the production of a scaled-up recipe. When a recipe is scaled up, the amount of each ingredient is increased to produce the amount of mixture that will yield the number of products required

- the use of ingredients in the correct proportions. The proportion of one ingredient to another must be the same as that in a one-off production
- the potential for producing varieties of shapes, sizes and flavours from the basic mix. The scaled-up mixture may be used to produce a variety of products
- the need to save time and labour. It takes very little extra time and energy to produce a large amount of a mixture. This has an economic spin-off in industry because it reduces labour and production costs
- the need for products to be of good quality and safe to eat. This principle is important in all food production. CCPs (see pages 12–13) are installed to check the quality and safety of products and monitor all aspects of a batch production system.

Spiced fruit buns

Ingredients
400g self-raising flour
1 level teaspoon
  baking powder
200g caster sugar
200g butter
4 eggs
Grated rind of 2 lemons
100g dried fruit
2 level teaspoons mixed spice

Equipment
1 large, 1 small mixing bowl
Scales and sieve
30 paper cake cases
2 X 12-hole and 1 X 6-hole
  tart tins
Grater, teaspoons
Beater, wooden spoon
  or mixer
Cooling tray

Method

1. Collect and weigh ingredients. Put cake cases in tart tins. Heat oven to gas mark 5 or 180°C.

2. Sieve flour, mixed spice and baking powder together into a small bowl. Grate lemons. Cream butter and sugar together in large bowl until soft. Beat in eggs a little at a time. Fold in flour mixture and mix gently to make a dropping consistency. Fold in dried fruit. Add a little milk if mixture is too dry.

3. Half-fill the cake cases with mixture.

4. Bake 15–20 minutes until risen and the centre of the cake springs back when pressed.

5. Cool on a cooling tray.

mass production

Pasta is an example of a product that can be made at home or in mass production. However, most pasta is bought by the consumer ready-made as a result of mass production.

Pasta is made from wheat and occupies a large proportion of the market demand for savoury cereal products. It is available in different forms, for example, dried, fresh or mixed with other ingredients to make composite products such as ravioli. The ingredients used are common to all types of pasta, but the huge variety of shapes available make it a very flexible food product. Its consumption is primarily associated with Italy, but it is now popular throughout the world.

Raw materials

The raw materials used in pasta production are water, eggs and wheat (from which the flour is made). The wheat used must be a particular type called durum wheat. This is a strong wheat containing a high proportion of protein, which will produce the required strength of dough for pasta production. The wheat is milled or ground to produce semolina, which is the coarsest grade of the starchy **endosperm**. The semolina grains produce a strong **gluten** network when mixed with water, which is able to stand up to the production processes of **extrusion** and **moulding** used to make pasta shapes.

Making pasta

Mass production of pasta covers the following processes:
1. The ingredients are selected and mixed in the required proportions. Eggs produce a richer dough, but are often missed out to reduce production costs. During this part of the process water is evenly distributed throughout the mixture and is absorbed by the semolina. In mass production the required proportions of the ingredients are measured into a large mixer, which operates mechanically to blend the ingredients together. Control points ensure that the conditions for mixing are correct. They include periodic checking of the water source, the proportions of ingredients, the rate and time at which the mixing takes place, and the size of the semolina particles.
2. The dough is kneaded, which makes it stick together. In mass production this process is carried out mechanically

▼ *A grain of wheat cut lengthwise.*

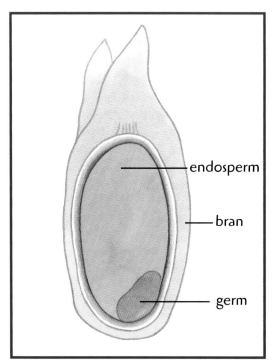

endosperm

bran

germ

▲ *Pasta shapes are made through an extruder and die.*

using a large paddle type of spoon. This action allows the gluten network to develop, thus giving the dough the required elastic quality. It is the protein content of the wheat that produces gluten when mixed with water. The control points cover the consistency required to ensure that efficient extrusion and/or rolling can take place.

3. The dough is shaped. This is carried out by extrusion of the dough through dies or casts. Commercial extruders consist of an extrusion worm, like the Archimedes screw, and a cylinder. The dough moves along the grooves of the screw towards the die or cast which is going to make the required shape. Control points cover the shape and size required and also limit the amount of heat energy produced during the process. If the dough is heated too much, the starch forms a gelatinous, or gluey, mass and there is a risk of ending up with a sticky product.

The quality of pasta

The quality of the protein and starch and the size of the semolina particles affect the degree to which the dough absorbs water. If the particles are too small, a sticky, liquid dough results. If the particles are too large, not all the flour is hydrated (takes in water). This causes difficulties at the extrusion stage, since the dough will be of variable consistency and some of it will not extrude, thus causing a halt in the system.

Evaluating pasta

The main **criterion** that consumers are looking for when assessing the quality of pasta is its **mouth-feel**, that is, its bite and consistency when cooked. The best pasta is one which is not too hard nor too sticky or soft when cooked. In Italian this quality of mouth-feel is called *al dente*, which literally means 'to the tooth'. Additional criteria are used in industry for evaluating pasta and pasta products. These include aroma, colour and appearance.

continuous-flow production

When large quantities of the same product are being made in industry, a continuous production line is set up. This results in a continuous flow of production from the selection of raw materials, through the manufacturing process to the packaging and distribution of the products.

The aim is to make identical products with little or no variation in weight, appearance, colour and so on. The product **specification** and criteria for development and manufacture are central to the successful running of a continuous production line system. This means that when the consumer is making a repeat purchase, the product is the same as it was the last time they bought it. The manufacture of cornflakes is a very good example of how successful a continuous production system can be.

> ## The story of cornflakes
>
> Dr John Harvey Kellogg was chief physician at the Battle Creek Sanatorium in Michigan, USA. He wanted to develop an easy-to-digest breakfast for the patients in the sanatorium. He worked on the development with his brother, who was the business manager of the sanatorium, and the result of their work was a paper-thin, malt-flavoured, toasted flake of the cereal maize, which became known as the cornflake.

▼ *A continuous-flow production line is set up for products such as cornflakes, where consistency is vital.*

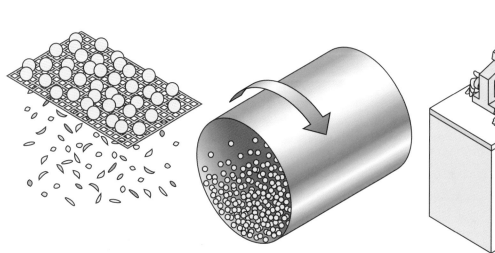

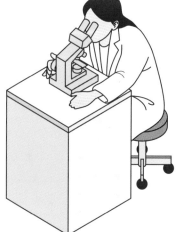

Milling is carried out to remove parts of the maize that would impair taste.

Malt, sugar and salt are added. The mixture is placed in giant cookers and rotated under steam pressure. The maize is then exposed to purifying hot air currents to reduce the level of moisture.

All levels of the production process are quality controlled.

Computer control

The selection and preparation of the materials, gathering them together (called assembly), and cooking are all part of the process that is usually carried out by automated machines controlled by microprocessors. Instructions for the programming of the microprocessors are contained in the production schedule and are developed to suit the product being manufactured. The following features of the process are part of the information which will be used in the programming of the microprocessor:
- the three temperature zones start at 200°C and reduce through 190 to 180°C
- the speed of the conveyor belt ensures the required amount of time is spent in each cooking zone

- the products need to be moved rapidly from the oven to a blast chiller where they are quickly cooled, to provide a temperature in which **micro-organisms** do not thrive.

The weighing information is given as percentages of the whole. Each ingredient is listed according to the proportion in which it should be used. The proportions for a quiche pastry, for example, are given as:

flour	60%
fat	30%
water	10%

These proportions are used to work out the formulation for the pastry, that is, the amounts of each ingredient that must be weighed out to produce the amount of pastry required.

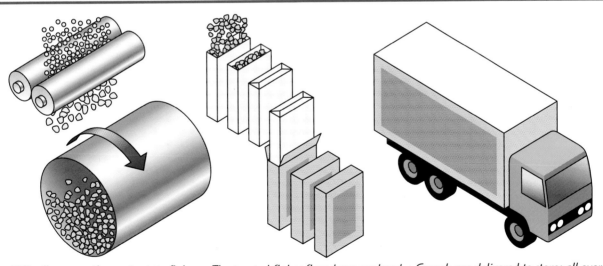

Mill rollers press the maize into flakes under 40 tons of pressure.
The flakes are toasted in giant rotary ovens.

The toasted flakes flow down enclosed tubes to machines where they are automatically dispensed by weight into the inner liners.
Filled liners of cereal are passed along conveyor belts and packed into cereal cartons.

Cereals are delivered to stores all over the country.

computer aided design

Computers are essential in many areas of the food industry. They are vital to designers and their teams. Computer aided design (CAD) is used extensively in food product design.

What does CAD do?

CAD involves using sophisticated computer packages to put information into a visual form. There are a number of activities which can be carried out using CAD packages. The main advantage is that the design of products, systems and packaging can first be modelled on the computer to see how viable it is without spending too much money.

Making an orange juice carton

The design of a new orange juice carton can be carried out using a CAD package. The different designs can be shown as three-dimensional or two-dimensional drawings. From these design drawings the computer can provide information about aspects of the design, such as the surface area or volume of the carton. An analysis of any stress that would be placed on the carton can also be provided.

Once a carton design has been chosen, the computer can produce a plan of it. This can be used to calculate the most efficient way of making the carton so that as little as possible of the material used to make the cartons is wasted.

The design team is often **networked** together, which means that everyone can see the developments each member of the team is producing. It is easier then to assess the viability of the whole design before expensive stages of production take place. The design may be checked for its effectiveness for holding the orange juice. A **prototype** may be tested against the juice **specification** to make sure it is leak-proof, pours easily and is of a suitable shape and size for convenient storage. A plan of the carton can be produced using a graphics program or desk-top publishing (DTP) package. The plan is printed and cut out and the package is assembled.

The packaging is evaluated and if it is found that it needs improvements, further designing takes place to incorporate them. If the improved carton is satisfactory it can go forward for production.

A specification for efficient production, filling and packaging of such a carton is compiled usually by a team of systems engineers. It is checked to make sure it meets all the criteria of the specification and when found satisfactory it can be transmitted by the computer to the appropriate manufacturing systems.

Modelling

Sometimes designers generate ideas using a CAD package on a computer to simulate designs, processes and systems. This gives the designer an accurate idea of how a design might look and how effective a system or a process might be.

Other uses of modelling

Designers of food products and packaging may need to find the best way to present **nutritional** information and other information about the ingredients from which a product is made. Specific databases are available which provide this information. By accessing a database, a

▲ *This is an example of computer aided design (CAD). CAD is used in many branches of engineering and manufacture, including those involved in food production.*

designer can:
- identify the relevant foods or ingredients, ask the database specific questions in order to get the relevant information, print out the answers and use them to improve the projected design
- compile a spreadsheet showing the whole nutritional value of the product.

CAD will then be used to discover the best way to present the information on a package. For example, CAD could be used to:
- compare different ways and forms of presenting nutritional information in the form of spreadsheets or charts. The information is presented visually, which makes it much easier to work with. These can be printed out or incorporated into a bigger document using a DTP package for presentation to the rest of the product design team
- cost a design. An ingredient price database provides the information which can then be presented on a spreadsheet, from which the whole cost of the product can be calculated
- produce different costings of a number of designs in order to compare them
- compare the appearance of different designs. The picture of the product can be drawn on the computer which can then generate different designs, colours and finishes. Each can be printed out in order to evaluate its effect.

computer aided manufacture

Consumer satisfaction is closely related to product quality. This means the product must be:

- safe to eat
- nutritious
- appetizing and tasty
- appealing
- good value for money
- convenient.

The most important aspect of a food product is always that it is safe to eat, though the order of importance in which the consumer places the other aspects varies according to circumstances and food product. It is in the context of the need to produce large quantities of safe, good quality food as quickly and cheaply as possible that computer aided manufacture (CAM) has developed.

▼ *This is a system for the production of cook-chill ready meals. The quality and safety of the raw materials, and the cooking, cooling and distribution temperatures are crucial aspects in the safe production of these meals. Control systems connected to a computer are calibrated (programmed) so that all the requirements are met automatically.*

Logistics

The production of safe food is a huge operation. The need to deliver the appropriate raw materials and goods to all people involved in this operation is of paramount importance. Other aspects involved include the movement of ingredients and products within the production system, the delivery of finished products to the point of sale and from there to the consumer. The overall term used to describe this operation is **logistics**. CAM is used extensively to achieve the required level of success at an acceptable cost throughout the whole operation.

What is involved in CAM?

CAM is used to ensure that manufacturing systems run efficiently throughout food production processes. For example, when ingredients are being mixed and must be kept at a specific temperature, the relevant information can be fed into a computer which operates controls within the system to ensure the required temperature is maintained.

The volume of production in the food industry is huge. Production on such a large scale requires both solids and liquids to flow into and away from items of equipment during the manufacture of food products. This is achieved by continuous flow processes in a large manufacturing plant (see pages 22–23). CAM is used to control the speed, direction, volume, temperature and

Large scale manufacture of bread is regulated by computer controls.

timing of these flow processes. For example, when pastry tarts are produced, all the equipment required and manufacturing systems used to produce the pastry, roll it, cut out the shapes, bake the pastry shapes and then fill them are programmed appropriately and can be controlled by a central computer.

The equipment that measures the amount of flour, fat and water to make the pastry is programmed to deposit exactly that amount into the mixing machine at the right time. The machine that puts the jam into the cases is also programmed so that each tart is filled with just the right amount of jam. This ensures that each tart is adequately filled but there is no risk of jam spilling out during cooking.

On a large scale

CAM is used in the large-scale manufacture of bread. Large bakeries produce many different types of bread and it is CAM that allows all the types to be handled through the same system. How does this work? The amount and type of flour, the temperature of the ovens and the cooling times are all regulated by the push of a button.

Print-outs are issued from the computer at regular intervals. The system is periodically checked by an engineer to make sure the system is within tolerance and has no faults.

The computer ensures that the production activities occur in the correct sequence. For example, in the production of plain white loaves the sequence is as follows:

- supply and quality of wheat are checked
- wheat made into flour, which is delivered to the bakery
- ingredients are measured
- ingredients are mixed, dough is shaped
- dough is proved (left to rise) at the appropriate temperature
- bread is baked
- bread is cooled, packed and delivered to point of sale.

good-quality food

How is quality in food products achieved? There are two related aspects concerned with the production of good-quality food. They are quality assurance and quality control.

Quality assurance involves identifying problems that might occur in the food production process, and putting control systems in place to make sure that the final product is of the right quality. Quality control involves testing the end product to ensure that it does meet the required standard.

How is quality assured?

The starting point is the setting of standards which a product must achieve. These are identified by the design team and include details of the manufacturing process. They are listed in a **specification** for the product which the manufacturer must follow and build into the production systems. The quality elements include safety and sensory requirements. Sensory requirements refers to what the product must look like, taste like and so on. Ongoing checks for quality take place in laboratories, **test kitchens** and at certain points in the production process.

The manufacturing process is set up so that all the required standards will be met. Then the product is monitored during and at the end of the process, to make sure that standards are maintained throughout. This happens in a number of ways, including:
- careful measuring of ingredients and random sampling to make sure the amounts are within the **tolerance** agreed

Quality checks are made at all stages of production.

Quality control means checking that the final product matches its specification.

- the addition of other materials to increase the quality of the finished product. Examples include emulsifiers, which stop ingredients separating out. The amount has to be carefully controlled – too much will spoil the product, too little will not be effective
- careful checking of consistencies so that the desired result is obtained. An example here is the covering of a cake, biscuit or sweet with chocolate. The chocolate must flow in order to cover the product but it must not be too runny or too thick, otherwise the covering will not be of good quality
- critical control points. For more information refer to pages 12–13.

Criteria

Quality assurance and quality control are achieved by careful planning and establishing specific **criteria** for the development and manufacture of a product.

If each activity has specific quality control criteria, such as those in the table shown below, it becomes more certain that good-quality and safe products are the result. The criteria must be detailed and comprehensive in order to achieve the degree of quality assurance and control which modern consumers take for granted.

Activity	Product	Quality control
Kneading bread dough	Plain white loaves	Observe nature of dough. Must be elastic, achieved by kneading for set length of time.
Mixing/blending one or more ingredients together, including a liquid	Sweet and savoury sauces, jellies, mousses	Observe to make sure nature of end product is correct, that is, smooth, even texture without lumps.
Controlling shape and form by extrusion	Biscuits, pasta	Observe and correct, if necessary, consistency. Ensure even pressure for uniform shape and size.

counting the cost

Consumers demand value for money when buying food products and generally want the price to be low. Food manufacturers and retailers want the opposite – that is, prices for products to be as high as possible. The manufacturers and retailers need to make a profit – they need to have money left over after all production and labour costs have been paid. The profit is used for further research and development, for improving facilities and for paying bonuses to shareholders who invest in companies.

Production costs

Costs involved in industrial food production include:
* finding, gathering and buying raw materials
* setting up production equipment and processes

* product design
* packaging and distribution
* advertising
* labour costs, including pension contributions and insurance
* maintenance of equipment and premises
* replacement of old or obsolete equipment
* testing, research and development.

Lowering costs

All the costs listed are essential but there are ways of reducing the costs of some items. The following are some cost-cutting strategies used in the industrial manufacture of some meat products:
* mix a more expensive meat with a similar but cheaper one – for example, beef pieces with minced beef in a meat pie

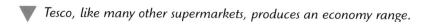

Tesco, like many other supermarkets, produces an economy range.

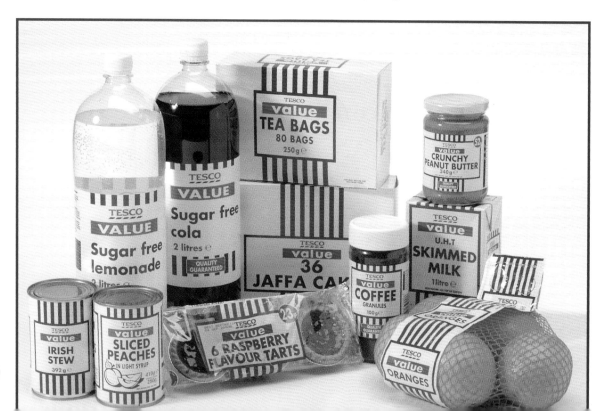

- decrease the amount of the more expensive ingredients used – for example, in a meat pie substitute vegetables for some of the meat. This must then be labelled as a meat and vegetable pie
- make a smaller product – for example, make a smaller and thinner fish-cake
- use extra water. Many beef products have chemicals added to them to make the products hold water. Hence a cheap burger that looks an acceptable size when raw will shrink when cooked
- use **re-formed** or **recovered** meat products that are extracted from the carcasses of animals by compressing the flesh and forcing any meat through a perforated metal drum
- reduce the amount and type of packaging – for example, most supermarkets have an economy food range, which is packed very simply and inexpensively.

The manufacturer has to weigh up the effect that these cost-cutting strategies may have on the finished product and their customers' satisfaction with it. If the quality of the products is significantly reduced then consumers will stop buying it.

A nut-free environment

Kinnerton Confectionery is one of the country's leading manufacturers of children's novelty and character confectionery. They specialize in making nut-free products, but have not always done so.

One day the managing director, Clive Beecham, received a telephone call from an angry mother complaining about a product based on a children's TV character which had a nut warning on the package. Clive Beecham explained that the warning was there not because the product contained nuts, but because it was produced in a factory where nut products were made. The result of this telephone call and comments from others about the same thing prompted him to invest over £1 million in dividing his factory into two distinct parts.

One zone was to be nut-free. Workers in the nut-free zone must communicate by mobile phone with those in the area where nuts are handled. They can move from one area to another only after washing and changing their clothes.

The company has separated its warehouse so that the nut packaging, moulds and work in progress are all kept in a special area. Colour-coded plastic pallets, bins, trays and other items have been specially bought. A positive air-flow system ensures that clean air always enters through the nut-free area and exits from the nut-contaminated area.

This is an example of a large financial investment within one company. It is unlikely that they will make a profit to start with because there is a limit to the price consumers will pay. However, in time the company may begin to profit from their commitment to producing nut-free products.

The example of bread production can be taken to show the type of equipment used in mass production (see pages 20–21) and continuous-flow (see pages 22–23) processes in the food industry.

▼ A large amount of bread is produced daily to keep up with consumer demand for the product. The industrial equipment used in a large-scale operation of bread production is shown here.

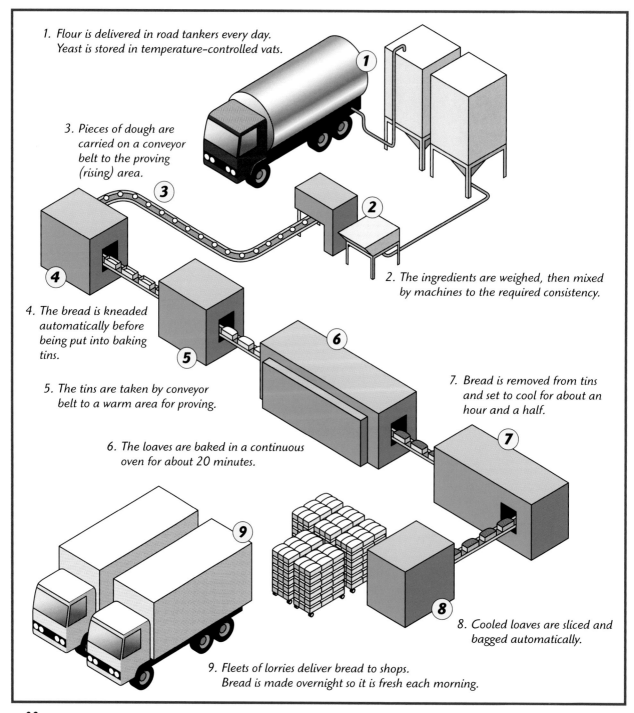

1. Flour is delivered in road tankers every day. Yeast is stored in temperature-controlled vats.

3. Pieces of dough are carried on a conveyor belt to the proving (rising) area.

2. The ingredients are weighed, then mixed by machines to the required consistency.

4. The bread is kneaded automatically before being put into baking tins.

5. The tins are taken by conveyor belt to a warm area for proving.

6. The loaves are baked in a continuous oven for about 20 minutes.

7. Bread is removed from tins and set to cool for about an hour and a half.

8. Cooled loaves are sliced and bagged automatically.

9. Fleets of lorries deliver bread to shops. Bread is made overnight so it is fresh each morning.

Pizza

Pizza producton makes use of similar processes to bread making. Commercial production of pizza is increasingly profitable because of the popularity of the many varieties of pizza. The production process covers:

- mixing and forming the dough
- cutting and pressing the dough to pizza bases of the same weight and thickness
- proving and baking
- cooling (and freezing if necessary)
- depanning the bases with a suction depanner
- decorating and packing.

The final product should have a good open texture, a crisp underside and a difference in **mouth-feel** between the topping and crust.

An Irish pizza company

An Irish firm invested heavily in improving their pizza plant in order to secure a larger market share. Their main aim was to produce a high-quality product that was slightly different from any other on the market. They decided on a product that would be sold frozen and that could be cooked on an open rack in a domestic oven. They developed four styles of pizza bases – deep-pan and thin, each one in both 15 cm and 23 cm diameters. They tested every hour during production to provide **feedback** about the effectiveness of the processing and to check quality control and safety were within tolerance limits. Samples were taken from the packaging area and baked in a laboratory at the factory.

During new product development which the company carries out on site it was discovered that there was a potential market for pizza sauces to match each pizza topping. The pizzas and sauces were manufactured, marketed and advertised as a completely new way of serving pizza at home. They provide what the company calls a complete 'flavour profile' and have proved very popular with consumers.

'Oven-fresh' products

Other bread products include 'fresh from the oven' bread and rolls. This concerns the production of pre-formed, yeast-raised baked goods that are stable at room temperature and that can be baked subsequently to give oven-fresh products. This is what happens in many supermarkets – the pre-formed products are delivered to the store and baked on site, giving rise to the appetising smell of baking bread in the shop. The system is called 'the Milton Keynes process' and has been revolutionary in generating sales of freshly baked bread. The system is patented, which means that it cannot be copied by a competitor.

stock control

Stock control rotation ensures that old stock is used before new stock.

The control of stock is a very important aspect of financially successful food production. Another important aspect is that all the ingredients required must be available at the time and place they are needed. However, it is a waste of money if more ingredients than are needed are available, because they either deteriorate or take up storage space. The two methods of stock control are just in time control, called JIT, and just in case control, called JIC.

JIC is rarely used now because it means that stock is taking up space and using finance with no return. JIT means that the item or a schedule – as in the delivery of products – can be available and produced in the correct amounts just at the time it is needed. This takes organization and planning, of which predicting what will be required in what quantities is a very important part. **Inventory** checks and counting stock are methods used to predict what will be required. It is similar to what happens in a domestic situation when someone makes a shopping list.

In a commercial situation, a hand stock control computer is often used. An operator enters the product being counted, usually with a specific code number for that product. Then the number unsold on the shelf is entered and sometimes the number to be ordered is also entered. All this information is transmitted to a central stock register either in the warehouse or on a computer in the store.

A reliable method of ordering new stock when required is also needed. This can be as simple as visiting a warehouse or phoning through an order in the case of a small manufacturer or retailer. Large manufacturers and retailers use a computerized inventory system linked to a delivery system.

Stock control rotation

Stock rotation means that the oldest stock must be used first, the next oldest next and so on. If stock rotation is organized effectively it means that everything is used whilst it is good quality and within its sell-by, use-by or best-before date.

Storing stock

When storing stock:
- appropriate conditions must be provided throughout all stages of storage. The conditions must fit the products. For example, some items must be stored in a dry and airy environment, whereas others must be stored at a specific temperature. Products requiring cold or refrigerated conditions must be transported in refrigerated lorries that provide the required temperature, and transferred immediately to either storage or sales environments that are also of the required temperature (such as a shop freezer or a chill cabinet)
- organized storage, so that the products that are first in are stored so that they will be used first
- clean and hygienic storage environments. Storage areas must be clean and free from the risk of vermin and insect infestation.

Large retailers

In the case of large retailers and manufacturers deliveries of stock must be based on what is used or sold and needs replacing. Taking a large supermarket company as an example, sales patterns, special sales promotions, particular seasons of the year, television cookery programmes, sales projections and so on are used to predict what is needed. This information can be transferred by computer from the store to head office and then to the warehouse nearest to the store. As mentioned above, the information is sometimes transmitted straight to the warehouse from the store.

Small retailers and manufacturers

Most small retailers and manufacturers use a computerized system to check their needs and keep an account of stock in hand. However, some still count the stock themselves and note what is required by hand. When they need to replace or order new stock, a number of methods may be used. These include buying from a 'cash and carry' store and transporting the products themselves, ordering the products from a wholesaler by telephone, email, fax or order form sent by post.

They may also follow some of the procedures discussed above in relation to monitoring their sales. As a result they may adjust the number and type of products they stock to fit in with circumstances such as the seasons of the year and festivals like Christmas and Easter.

food laws and regulations

Regulations concerning food apply to any business concerned with food production and retailing, including restaurants, manufacturers of food products, street vendors, corner shops, garages and supermarkets. The only time the regulations do not apply is when food is cooked at home for private consumption.

Primary legislation

The primary legislation on the safety of food is the Food Safety Act 1990. This act provides a flexible framework for food law. It concentrates on the basic issues and does not go into great detail on matters such as food quality or food labelling and advertising. These details are dealt with in subsidiary regulations.

The Food Safety Act 1990

This is a wide-ranging law which is stronger than any previous laws on food safety and consumer protection in the food sector. The act has built upon previous laws and updated them, and has introduced other particular features. Its aims are to:
- continue to ensure that all food produced for sale is safe to eat, reaches quality expectations and is not misleadingly presented
- provide legal powers and penalties
- enable the UK to fulfil its responsibilities in the European Community
- keep pace with technological change.

(From 'The Food Safety Act 1990 and You', Advice from HM Government.)

What is covered by the act?

A broad range of food-related commercial activities are covered. These include food sources, such as crops and animals, articles that come into contact with food (so-called contact materials), such as cling film, and manufacturing equipment, such as mixing vats.

What does the Act mean by 'food'?

In law the word 'food' has a wider meaning than in everyday use. It covers:
- anything used as a food ingredient including additives, such as colourings, sweeteners and preservatives
- animals eaten live, such as oysters
- drink
- products like slimming aids and dietary supplements
- water used in food production or drawn from the tap in the course of a food business.

What about food sources?

The Act covers crops and live animals and any food made from them. This means that farmers are directly affected by food law. Under the Act most farmers are considered to be running food businesses. One exception to this is when a farmer rears animals and sells them live.

Inspection of food sources

People called enforcement officers can inspect food sources when they think it is appropriate. For example, there are regulations that control traces of veterinary medicines in animals, meat

Farmer talking to an inspector from the Department for Environment, Food and Rural Affairs. ▶

and meat products. If an enforcement officer suspects that food about to enter the human food chain contains traces, the officer can inspect the food source at any time without giving warning.

These inspectors have power to take action on-farm when they find that:

- illegal growth-promoting hormones or unlicensed substances have been used
- maximum medicine residue levels in meat have been exceeded through farmers failing to observe 'withdrawal' periods prior to slaughter when all medications should cease
- records of the administration of veterinary medicines to farm animals have not been kept.

How does the Act affect food importers?

There are no longer import controls on food brought in from other EC member states, because we are all in a single market. If, however, the food comes from third-world countries, food importers have to comply with the Imported Food Regulations 1984 or the provisions of product-specific hygiene regulations when the products are of animal origin.

Who is responsible for enforcing the Act?

It is enforced by both central and local government. Central government oversees the work of local authorities. It has an advisory role, particularly in relation to the issuing of statutory codes of practice. Its main task, however, is to develop food policy and work with the European Community in relation to food law.

The Food Standards Agency, which came into being in April 2000, deals with protection of consumer rights and aids the government in the writing of legislation concerning food. The mission of the agency is to be 'open and transparent'.

Local government authorities are responsible for enforcing food law in two areas. They are:

- food labelling, composition and any instances of **chemical** contamination – dealt with by trading standards officers
- food hygiene matters, **microbiological** contamination of food and food which for whatever reason is unfit for human consumption – dealt with by environmental health officers.

It is the duty of all people involved in food production to understand and follow all the health and safety requirements that are relevant to the production of food and the safety of everyone working in the process.

Training and qualifications

It is important for all members of staff to be trained about hygienic practices in order that each one can deal effectively with the potential hazards of the processes in which they are involved. The Basic Food Hygiene Certificate is the first level qualification in food hygiene. It is universally recognized in the food industry. The Chartered Institute of Environmental Health (CIEH) awards a certificate to those who are successful. The course gives food handlers the knowledge and understanding that are essential for good hygienic working practices. It covers such things as personal hygiene, storage of food and control of pests and waste.

The work of the local authority

Local authorities have certain powers under the law to inspect, check, test and approve products, equipment and ingredients. Two types of officer are involved in this work. Trading standards officers deal with cases of chemical

An environmental officer checking that a refrigerator is at the correct temperature.

contamination of food, food contents and labelling. They are also responsible for checking and inspecting animal slaughterhouses. Environmental officers deal with hygiene, **microbiological** contamination of food and foods which are unfit for human consumption.

Both these types of officer have a lot of power and can close all or part of a business down, be it a shop, factory or a food company, if there is a serious breach of regulations which is not speedily rectified. The officers have the right to enter and inspect food premises at all reasonable hours – they do not have to make a prior appointment. The other aspects of health and safety concern everyone involved in the process of production. All aspects of any food premise must comply with rigorous installation and maintenance procedures. All equipment must have safety controls and clear instructions for safe use. Employees must be supplied with any appropriate safety equipment. Working areas must be free from obstacles and all equipment and materials to do with the production process must be stored safely when not in use.

Safe catering

Any manager or owner of a catering or other food business must satisfy consumers' demands and expectations for the food they order to be at the right temperature, look appetising, taste good and be good value for money. However, above all it must be safe to eat.

▼ *This is an example of an assured safe catering system issued by the Department of Health:*

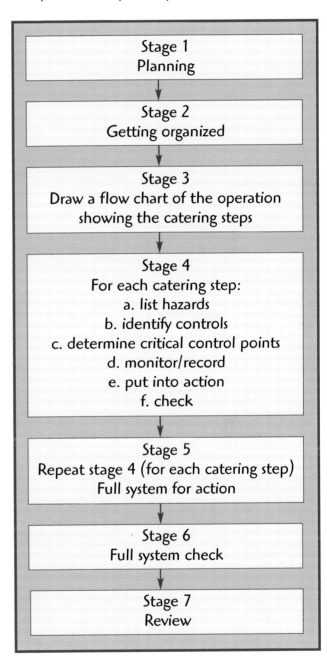

Stage 1
Planning

Stage 2
Getting organized

Stage 3
Draw a flow chart of the operation showing the catering steps

Stage 4
For each catering step:
a. list hazards
b. identify controls
c. determine critical control points
d. monitor/record
e. put into action
f. check

Stage 5
Repeat stage 4 (for each catering step)
Full system for action

Stage 6
Full system check

Stage 7
Review

working hygienically

It is necessary to work hygienically whatever the scale of production so that food is produced and supplied safe to eat. All food producers must follow hygienic work practices in order to avoid:
- infestation by pests
- spoilage of food
- production loss and loss of business
- food poisoning
- complaints from consumers and retailers, possibly leading to legal action.

Food regulations

The Food Safety (General Food Hygiene) Regulations (1995) and the European Community Food Hygiene Directive (93/43EEC) ensure common food hygiene rules across the European Community. The regulations aim to set out basic hygiene principles. They have a stronger focus than previous regulations on how to identify and control food safety risks at each stage of preparing and selling food. In addition, specific regulations exist that must be followed in the production of basic commodities, such as meat, milk, fish and poultry. Everyone involved in food production and retailing must follow the appropriate regulations for a particular operation. All the processes involved are covered, including:
- preparation methods, such as peeling and chopping
- manufacturing processes
- special processes, such as pasteurization
- distribution
- transport
- handling processes, such as in a sandwich bar

- selling, as in a shop, supermarket or from a vending machine
- packaging
- storage.

Anyone who processes or sells food and is covered by the Food Safety (General Hygiene) Regulations 1995 is legally bound to ensure that all operations are carried out safely and hygienically. This means that in all operations the following are crucial aspects:
- the identification of hazards which put food safety at risk
- identification of high and low areas of risk
- installing, maintaining, monitoring and reviewing safety controls.

The HACCP system is most commonly used to identify hazards and install controls (see pages 12–13).

What else is important?

The equipment used in food production must, by law, meet certain criteria. It must be:
- non-toxic, non-absorbent and resistant to rusting to prevent contamination
- movable for easy and rigorous cleaning
- be in perfect condition, that is, no chips, flaking of surfaces and so on.

Staff must know exactly what cleaning must be done and the methods and materials to use. A cleaning schedule must include reference to:
- all the surfaces that come into contact with food, such as chopping boards and knives

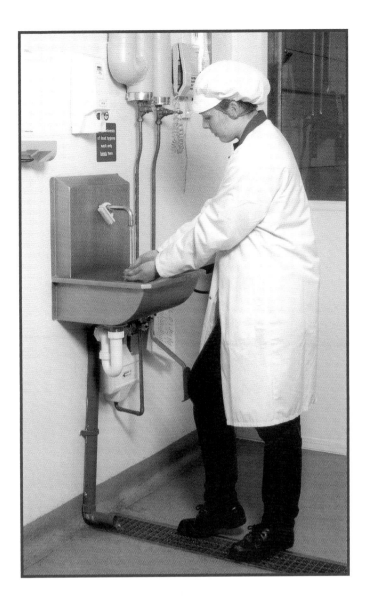

This person is washing their hands at a specially designed system. Notice the hands do not touch the tap – it is turned on by pressing a lever under the basin with the knee.

- surfaces that are touched by hands, such as cupboard doors, refrigerator handles and oven doors
- they should empty waste bins frequently and keep them covered.

The law also requires anyone handling food to take personal responsibility to guard against food becoming contaminated. There must be very strict rules about personal hygiene. They must cover:

- the face, for instance earrings must be removed and there must be no spitting, coughing, biting of nails, chewing, smoking or tasting of food (unless it is part of the job)
- washing, including washing hands after using the lavatory
- hands, including the fact that rings should not be worn and that gloves should be used when necessary
- clothes – the need to wear protective clothing including a hat, hair net, an overall, appropriate covering for feet, which may be colour-coded rubber boots. The covering must not be open-toed and must be different from that worn for travel to and from work.
- skin, with reference to cuts and wounds, which must be covered with a blue waterproof dressing. This sometimes has a metal strip though it, so that it can be detected by a metal detector in a production line if it accidentally drops into the food
- illnesses of any kind, which, by law, must be reported to the company
- the need to report any overseas travel.

Generally, the food hygiene regulations cover the following:

- clean water supplies with facilities for washing utensils, food and equipment. Hot and cold running water at kitchen sinks and hand basins
- provision of soap, nail brushes and hand-drying facilities at hand basins
- lighting, ventilation, organization of all rooms and sites
- minimum standards of design, layout and hygiene that must be met
- provision of storage facilities for employees' belongings
- siting of lavatories and washrooms separately from food storage areas.

the future

Food will always be needed. However, in the western world demands for new food products will probably continue to increase. In developing countries, where food supply is not as plentiful, the demands will focus on the need to supply enough basic, nutritious foods to make sure no one is hungry and ill as a result of shortage of food. This is not as easy as it sounds.

New developments

The world's population is increasing but the land available for the production of food is not expanding to the same extent. It is believed that the populations of the less developed countries will increase by about two and a half times, the situation not stabilizing until about the year 2050. One solution is to improve the yield of various crops. There are now new strains of crop being developed which have been **genetically modified** to be more disease- and pest-resistant, giving a greater yield than before.

Another development is the emergence of a completely new, artificial cereal. It is called triticale, a name made up from *triticum* (Latin for wheat) and *secale* (Latin for rye). Experiments have shown high yields of the grain in poor conditions. This may mean it can help increase food supply in developing countries. It is rich in protein and makes a very good version of unleavened (unrisen) bread.

Farming techniques are changing, too. Methods have been developed to produce crop yields three times greater than would be yielded from traditional methods of cultivation.

Fair return

It is said that annually over a third of the total world production of cereals is fed to animals. Some scientists believe that we get a very poor return for this. On average, for a person to gain just one calorie from an animal product, for example milk, the animal would have to have eaten 7 vegetable calories. This is called indirect consumption. However, if a person eats a vegetable, no calories will be lost. This is called direct consumption.

Biotechnology

Modern biotechnology involves understanding and making changes in the characteristics of living things. People are often suspicious of products made through biotechnology, fearing that they are unsafe. However, the techniques are not new – they have actually been used to make products for a very long time. Fermentation, where **micro-organisms** such as yeasts and bacteria are used in food production, is an example of traditional biotechnology. Whilst it is right that the consumer should ask questions about the safety of products made as a result of biotechnology, it would also be helpful for them to have more information about biotechnological developments.

▲ Some developing countries use genetically modified crops because the yield is so much greater than ordinary crops.

Novel foods

A novel food is a food or food ingredient that has not been used previously for human consumption to a significant degree within the European Community. It includes foods containing, consisting of or produced from genetically modified organisms.

Increasingly the consumer is expecting more from a food product. Genetic modification can be used to meet these expectations. The development of a more flavoursome tomato is an example. During the softening part of the ripening process the action of various **enzymes** is involved. Modification of the genes of the tomato prevented the enzymes from working and allowed the tomato to ripen on the vine for longer without going soft. This produced a tomato with a superior flavour.

What next?

There is no doubt that further investigation into new techniques of food production must take place, but it is also important to have a balanced view of future food production. The food industry needs to provide sufficient safe food for all. In the western world, however, this need is in competition with increasing consumer demand for more convenience, variety, and quality in food.

Ethical considerations

Some people are concerned that they may be eating food that has been genetically modified. Committees have been set up to monitor the ethical issues of techniques used to breed farm animals, including those that use gene technology. There are also labelling requirements to ensure that the consumer of a food product is informed about composition, **nutritional** value, and the presence of allergy-causing or genetically modified ingredients.

resources

Books

Collins Real World Food Technology J Inglis & S Plews with E Chapman	Collins 1997	
Collins Study & Revision Guide: Food Technology GCSE J Hotson & J Robinson	Collins 1999	
Examining Food Technology Anne Barnett	Heinemann 1996	
Food Technology Janet Inglis, Sue Plews, Eileen Chapman	Collins Educational 1997	
Food Technology to GCSE Anita Tull	Oxford University Press 1998	
GCSE Food Technology for OCR Jenny Ridgwell	Heinemann 1999	
Nuffield D&T: Food Technology	Longman 1996	
The Science and Technology of Foods R K Proudlove	Forbes Publications	
Skills in Food Technology Jenny Ridgwell	Heinemann 1997	
Understanding Ingredients Anne Barnett	Heinemann 1998	

Contacts

The Bakers' Federation
6 Catherine Street
London WC2 5JJ
www.bakersfederation.org.uk
Gives information on cereals, baking,
bread and flour.

British Nutrition Foundation
High Holborn House
52-54 High Holborn
London WC1V 6RQ
020 7404 6504
www.nutrition.org.uk

The Flour Advisory Bureau
21 Arlington Street
London SW1A 1RN
www.fabflour.co.uk
Provides resources about bread and flour.

The Food & Drink Industry National
Training Organisation
6 Catherine Street
London WC2 5JJ
020 7836 2460
www.foodanddrinknto.org.uk
More information on training and careers
in food and drink manufacturing.

The Institute of Food Science &
Technology
5 Cambridge Court
210 Shepherd's Bush Rd
London
W6 7NJ
020 7603 6316
www.ifst.org
Gives information on food-related
training and careers.

Sustain (previously The National Food
Alliance)
5-11 Worship Street
London
EC2A 2BH
020 7628 7774
Publications focus on food and its
production, looking at how food is grown,
manufactured, transported and stored.

I.C.T

www.flourandgrain.com
New education site from The Flour
Advisory Bureau and The Home Grown
Cereals Authority.

www.foodforum.org.uk
Useful for general information about
food, diet and health.

www.foodtech.org.uk
A site for students as well as teachers that
gives a good overview of food technology.

glossary

biotechnology the use of biological processes in food production; in particular, the production of specific qualities in plants and animals by genetic modification

calibrated to insert a gauge or measurement into an instrument and/or a piece of machinery in order that it operates effectively

central processing unit a piece of computerized equipment which controls all the aspects of a whole system

citric acid a sharp tasting crystalline acid; present in the juice of lemons and other sour fruits; it is also manufactured commercially

competitor a person or organization who is engaged in commercial or economic competition with others

compressed air air that is at more than atmospheric pressure

concave a surface which curves inwards

contact material a material which touches another and allows a particular action to take place

criteria a list of principles or standards by which something may be judged or decided

endosperm the part of a seed which acts as the food store for the embryo of a developing plant

enzyme a substance produced by a living organism which acts as a catalyst to promote a specific biochemical reaction

extrusion to shape a material by forcing it through a die

feedback information given in relation to the operation of a machine or a system. The modification or control of a process or system by its results or effects.

fructose a sugar, found especially in honey and fruit

genetically modified the deliberate alteration of the characteristics of an organism by manipulating its genetic material

glucose an elastic, stretchy substance produced when the wheat proteins, gliadin and glutenin are mixed with water

gluten a protein found in wheat

inventory a complete list of items, such as goods in stock

invert sugar a mixture of glucose and fructose obtained by the hydrolysis of sucrose

logistics the detailed coordination of a large and complex operation

market research the activity of gathering information about consumers' needs and preferences

microbiological the scientific study concerned with micro-organisms

micro-organism an organism so small that it can only be seen with a microscope

moulding to form shapes from malleable substances

network a group or system of interconnected people or things

nutritional full of nutrients; nourishing

one-off made or carried out only once. A unique operation.

open-loop a system where information passes in one direction only, for example from input to output of a system

optic fibre a thin glass fibre through which light can be transmitted

pectin a soluble polysaccharide present in ripe fruits; used as a setting agent for jams and jellies

pH the measurement of acidity or alkalinity of a substance

protein a class of nitrogenous compounds which form part of the body tissues and are important in a healthy diet

prototype a first or preliminary form from which other forms are developed or copied

recovered as in recovered meat. This involves extracting meat from the carcasses of animals by compressing the flesh and scraping the bones.

scaling-up increasing the scale of a formulation to produce a greater number of products

specification the detailed description of the design and materials used to make something

sucrose the chief component of cane or beet sugar

test kitchen a kitchen where formulations and products are produced, analysed and tested (including modifications if necessary)

tolerance an allowable amount of variation of a specified quantity

unleavened product made without yeast or other raising agent

user interface the parts of a system used by people, for example, the counter of a shop

vacuum a space or container from which air has been completely or partly removed

viscosity the degree to which a mixture moves and/or is thickened

index